AF270619

Fairies

by Grace Hansen

WORLD OF MYTHICAL BEINGS

Abdo Kids Jumbo is an Imprint of Abdo Kids
abdobooks.com

abdobooks.com

Published by Abdo Kids, a division of ABDO, P.O. Box 398166, Minneapolis, Minnesota 55439.
Copyright © 2024 by Abdo Consulting Group, Inc. International copyrights reserved in all countries.
No part of this book may be reproduced in any form without written permission from the publisher.
Abdo Kids Jumbo™ is a trademark and logo of Abdo Kids.

Printed in the United States of America, North Mankato, Minnesota.

102023

012024

THIS BOOK CONTAINS
RECYCLED MATERIALS

Photo Credits: Alamy, Everette Collection, Getty Images, Shutterstock

Production Contributors: Teddy Borth, Jennie Forsberg, Grace Hansen
Design Contributors: Candice Keimig, Pakou Moua

Library of Congress Control Number: 2023937672
Publisher's Cataloging-in-Publication Data

Names: Hansen, Grace, author.

Title: Fairies / by Grace Hansen

Description: Minneapolis, Minnesota : Abdo Kids, 2024 | Series: World of mythical beings | Includes online
resources and index.

Identifiers: ISBN 9781098268572 (lib. bdg.) | ISBN 9781098269272 (ebook) | ISBN 9781098269623
(Read-to-Me ebook)

Subjects: LCSH: Fairies--Juvenile literature. | Mythical animals--Juvenile literature. | Folklore--Juvenile
literature. | Legends--Juvenile literature.

Classification: DDC 398.2454--dc23

Table of Contents

The Myth of the Fairy

Fairies are mythical beings. They have been a part of **folklore** for thousands of years. The earliest stories mainly come from Europe.

In Greek mythology, gods and
goddesses created creatures
to care for the earth. These
creatures were small and
beautiful. Some were good
and some were evil.

The First Fairies

In the early 1200s, Englishman Gervase of Tillbury wrote *Otia Imerpialia*. In it, Gervase describes magical creatures called fairies. Fairies could be large or small, good or evil, beautiful or ugly.

The English people came to fear fairies. They believed that fairies could **curse** them. Many refused to even say the word "fairy" out loud.

Famous Fairies of Fiction

In 1605, William Shakespeare **debuted** his play *A Midsummer Night's Dream*. It features several fairies. Puck is one of the main fairy characters. He enjoys playing harmless pranks.

People soon understood that
fairies were not real. More
writers began to include good
fairies in their stories. Many of
these characters are known and
loved today.

In 1697, French author Charles Perrault published a collection of fairy tales. It included the stories *The Sleeping Beauty in the Woods* and *Cinderella*. Both stories have magical and caring fairies. These characters became known as fairy godmothers.

In 1902, Scottish writer J.M.
Barrie introduced the character
Peter Pan. Peter's best friend is
a fairy named Tinker Bell. Tinker
Bell is **feisty** and plays tricks.
But she is also very **loyal**.

Fairies Today

What fairies represent has changed a lot over the years. Today, they continue to inspire people with their beauty and wonder.

Modern Fairies Based in Mythology

Flora, Fauna, And Merryweather
Sleeping Beauty

- Three fairy godmothers
- Tasked with caring for the King's daughter, Aurora
- Use their magical abilities to help Aurora

The Tooth Fairy
Tooth Fairy movie

- Transported to the realm of the of tooth fairies
- Has wings to fly
- Has magical items such as shrinking paste and a wand

The Sugar Plum Fairy
The Nutcracker And the Four Realms

- Lives in the Land of Sweets
- Has wings to fly
- Acts very sweet and kind at first, but really wants power and control

Glossary

curse – to cause to suffer.

debuted – presented to the public for the first time.

feisty – determined, spirited, or quick-tempered.

folklore – the stories and ways of a group of people from a certain place or country.

loyal – showing devotion and faithfulness to someone.

Index

Abdo Kids
ONLINE
FREE! ONLINE MULTIMEDIA RESOURCES

Visit **abdokids.com** to access crafts, games, videos, and more!